Joseph's Journey

Volume 4

A Look in My Rear View Mirror:
"Did I just Waste a Precious Life –
That Kept Mine from Being Used"

Joseph's Journey

Volume 4

A Look in My Rear View Mirror:
"Did I just Waste a Precious Life –
That Kept Mine from Being Used"

by

Joseph Fram

Everlasting Publishing
Vancouver, Washington USA

Joseph's Journey
Volume 4

A Look in My Rear View Mirror:
"Did I just Waste a Precious Life –
That Kept Mine from Being Used"

by
Joseph Fram

Library of Congress Control Number
2009902376

ISBN: 0-9778083-7-8
ISBN-13: 978-0-9778083-7-3

First Edition
Everlasting Publishing
P.O. Box 965
Vancouver, WA 98666-0965

Editor's Note:
I thank God for the opportunity to compile these poems into this 4th book for my dad, Joe Fram. Each poem draws me closer to him and lets me know a little bit more about what's going on inside this great man who is my earthly father.

I especially thank God for all these years with Dad and the love we share, which grows and grows, through the love of Jesus, which never ends.

Dana Fram Pride

I would like to dedicate this book to my mom and dad, who never had a chance to see the work of their son.

Joseph Fram

JOSEPH'S JOURNEY VOLUME 4

EACH DAY
by
Joseph Fram

EVERY DAY IS PRECIOUS
HOW OFTEN DO WE HEAR
WE DON'T PAY MUCH ATTENTION
UNTIL IT BECOMES A YEAR

WE TAKE EACH DAY FOR GRANTED
HOW MUCH OF IT DO WE WASTE
IF WE HAVE TIME FOR ENJOYMENT
WE DO IT IN SUCH HASTE

IF WE FILL EACH DAY WITH KINDNESS
IT BECOMES A PRECIOUS DAY
AND LOVE WILL SOON SURROUND US
CAN YOU THINK OF A BETTER WAY?

IF YOUR DAY HAS BEEN OFFENDED
BY ONE WHO HAS A BAD ONE TOO
DON'T LET IT RUIN THE WHOLE DAY
FIND SOMETHING FUN TO DO

SO EVERY DAY IS PRECIOUS
IF YOU HAVE TO QUESTION WHY
PERHAPS I KNOW THE REASON
IT'S ONE DAY CLOSER TILL YOU DIE

ALONE

by
Joseph Fram

THERE ARE THOSE TIMES
FOR MY JOY AND MY SAD
WHEN THINGS ALL GO RIGHT
OR THINGS ALL GO BAD

THE TIMES I WAS HAPPY
I CAN CLEARLY SEE
IT IS A VISION
I KEEP CLOSE TO ME

THERE ARE TIMES IN MY LIFE
I WOULD RATHER FORGET
WHEN THE HURT WAS SO BAD
I HAVEN'T GOTTEN OVER IT YET

AS I MEASURE THE BALANCE
I GUESS THINGS EVEN OUT
AT THIS STAGE IN MY LIFE
EVEN IS WHAT IT'S ABOUT

WHEN I AM WITHIN MYSELF
I AM NEVER ALONE
MY COMPANIONS ARE MY MEMORIES
AND SOME HEARTACHES I HAVE KNOWN

MEMORIES

by
Joseph Fram

MY MEMORIES ARE ALL IN TATTERS
DON'T KNOW WHICH ARE WRONG OR RIGHT
I TRY TO GRAB THEM IN A WINDSTORM
OR MAYBE IN THE DARK OF NIGHT

I SEE MY IMAGE IN THE MIRROR
SOMETIMES I WONDER WHO IT COULD BE
HOW DID I GET FROM THERE TO HERE
AND IS IT REALLY ME

DID I DO ALL THE THINGS I SEE
IN THE MEMORIES FROM THE PAST
OR WAS IT SOMEONE ELSE I SAW
THE TIME GOES BY SO FAST

DID I LOVE THEN LOVE AGAIN
OR IS ILLUSION JUST MY FATE
AND IF IT NEVER HAPPENED
FOR ME IS IT TOO LATE

MY MEMORIES AND MY PRESENT
LEAVE ME SOMEWHAT CONFUSED
DID I JUST WASTE A PRECIOUS LIFE
THAT KEPT MINE FROM BEING USED

3

DRIVING

by
Joseph Fram

DON'T YOU JUST HATE IT
WHEN YOU HAVE SOME PLACE TO GO
AND YOU GET BEHIND A DRIVER
WHO YOU THINK IS GOING SLOW

I ALWAYS THOUGHT THAT CARS
WERE BUILT MOSTLY FOR SPEED
BUT IF YOU CAN'T USE THE HORSEPOWER
A QUESTION ARISES ABOUT THE NEED

SOME DRIVE AT THE LIMIT
THEY DON'T SEEM TO CARE
THAT ALL THE PEOPLE BEHIND THEM
ARE IN A RUSH TO GET SOMEWHERE

BUT NOW THAT THE GAS PRICES
HAVE REACHED AN ALL TIME HIGH
I SLOW FOR THAT AND OTHER REASONS
I NOW WILL TELL YOU WHY

WHEN I REACHED MY DESTINATION
MY GAS TANK WAS NEAR THE TOP
SO I GUESS GOOD THINGS HAPPEN
WHEN YOU ARE FOLLOWING A COP

NO MATTER WHAT THE COST
by
Joseph Fram

I SAW HER LOOKING AT ME
SUCH SADNESS IN HER EYE
WE KNEW THE TIME HAD COME
WHEN SHE SAW ME CLOSE TO CRY

HER LIFE HAD TAKEN SUCH A TURN
YESTERDAY SHE WAS YOUNG AND STRONG
NOW SHE IS PLAGUED WITH MALADIES
WHEN EVERYTHING IS WRONG

HER HANDS THAT ONCE WERE STEADY
TREMBLE LIKE LEAVES TO A BREEZE
HER GAIT IS SLOW AND MEASURED
NOTHING COMES TO HER WITH EASE

HER MEMORY SOMETIMES FAILS HER
SHE TRIES SO HARD TO SEE
THE PICTURES IN HER MIND NOW
ARE A BLUR OF WHAT USED TO BE

BUT SHE IS STILL THE ONE I LOVE
NO MATTER WHAT THE COST
THE HAPPINESS SHE BROUGHT TO ME
IN MY WORLD CANNOT BE LOST

THE FLY
by
Joseph Fram

HAVE YOU EVER WATCHED A FLY
PLAY ITS LITTLE GAME
JUST WHEN YOU THINK IT'S SWATTED
IT APPEARS ELSEWHERE JUST THE SAME

IT THEN GOES TO A WINDOW
YOU THINK "I'VE GOT IT NOW"
WHEN YOU TAKE YOUR SWAT
IT GETS AWAY SOMEHOW

THEN IT TRIES TO TICKLE YOU
UNTIL IT DRIVES YOU MAD
WHEN YOU NEVER CAPTURE IT
I WONDER IF IT IS GLAD

WHEN YOU THINK "I'LL GO TO BED"
IT WILL WAIT UNTIL YOU REST
THEN IT WILL BUZZ YOUR NOSE
THAT IS THE ULTIMATE TEST

WHEN THE LIGHTS ARE PUT OUT
IT WILL FLY AWAY AND STAY
POISED SAFELY IN A CORNER
TO ANNOY YOU ANOTHER DAY

THINGS CHANGE
by
Joseph Fram

ALL THINGS CHANGE
SO I HAVE BEEN TOLD
IF YOU DISAGREE
THEY SAY YOU'RE GETTING OLD

SOME SAY OLDER IS WISER
OTHERS SAY "GET UP TO SPEED"
SOMETIMES WHEN ONE IS OLDER
SOMEONE SHOULD EXPLAIN THE NEED

IT WOULD BE SO SILLY
TO YEARN FOR HORSE AND BUGGY DAYS
OR DO AWAY WITH MODERN THINGS
THAT SURELY CHANGE OUR WAYS

BUT THERE ARE MANY THINGS
WE LEARNED SO LONG AGO
THAT SADDER THE WORLD WOULD BE
IF WE LET THEM GO

LIKE THE MORALS WE WERE TAUGHT
ABOUT RIGHTS AND FAIR PLAY
IF WE TRY TO CHANGE THESE THINGS
WE ARE BOUND TO LOSE OUR WAY

THANKSGIVING

by
Joseph Fram

DEAR LORD UP IN HEAVEN
BLESS THE FOOD ON THIS TABLE
WITH THANKS FOR THIS GATHERING
AND THANKS THAT WE ARE ABLE

THE HANDS THAT PREPARED THIS
THANK YOUR GUIDANCE AND YOUR CARE
AND THE PEOPLE YOU BROUGHT TOGETHER
FOR THIS FOOD TO SHARE

WITH YOUR HAND TO GUIDE US
YOU HAVE BROUGHT US ALL THIS FAR
AND ALL THAT WE HAVE
IS BECAUSE OF WHAT YOU ARE

WE KNOW WE SHOULD THANK YOU
EACH DAY OF THE YEAR
BUT ON THIS SPECIAL DAY
WE THANK YOU TO BE HERE

FOR THOSE NOT AMONG US
WE ALSO SHARE OUR LOVE
WITH ALL OF OUR DEAREST FRIENDS
AND WITH THOSE UP ABOVE

IF

by
Joseph Fram

IF I HAD ONLY
IS SOMETHING WE ALL SAY
ABOUT ONE THING OR ANOTHER
WE COULD DO SOME OTHER WAY

THERE ARE MANY IFS IN US
SOME WHICH MAKE US SAD
I WILL BET THEY ARE OUTWEIGHED
BY THE ONES THAT MAKE US GLAD

I HAVE GIVEN THOUGHT TO IFS
AND JUST WHAT THEY MIGHT MEAN
LIKE IF THERE WERE NO IFS
WOULD IT MAKE OUR LIFE MORE CLEAN

IF WE DWELL ON IFS
WOULD IT DRIVE US MAD
AND MAKE US DISCONTENTED
WITH ALL THE THINGS WE HAD

I BELIEVE GOD GIVES US IFS
SO FROM THEM WE CAN LEARN
THEN WE WON'T HAVE TO USE THEM
WHEN IT BECOMES OUR TURN

9

CHEAP ENOUGH
by
Joseph Fram

WHILE I WAS WATCHING TELEVISION
I HEARD AN EVANGELIST SAY
I CAN GET YOU INTO HEAVEN
AND YOU WON'T HAVE MUCH TO PAY

HE JUST WENT ON A TALKING
ABOUT HOW EVIL WE SEEM TO BE
BUT HE COULD CORRECT IT ALL
GOD GAVE HIM THE EYES TO SEE

WELL, I SHUDDERED AS I LISTENED
HOW WE ALL ARE GOING TO HELL
BUT THEN HE OFFERED US SOME HOPE
HE'D SOON TELL US HOW TO GET WELL

THEN HE SMILED INTO THE CAMERA
AND WITH THE EASE OF A MAGIC MAN
"SEND ME $40.00 ADMISSION TO HEAVEN
GOD AND I KNOW ALL OF YOU CAN"

I GAVE IT THOUGHT FOR QUITE A WHILE
MY LIFE HAS BEEN KIND OF ROUGH
SO I UP AND SENT HIM FORTY DOLLARS
SEEMS TO ME THAT'S CHEAP ENOUGH

SISTER'S LOVE
by
Joseph Fram

WHEN GOD INVENTED LOVE
HE KNEW YOU WOULD COME ALONG
THAT YOU WOULD DO ALL RIGHT
AND STAY AWAY FROM WRONG

YOU WOULD BE A FINE COMPANION
FOR ALL YOUR FAMILY
AND LET YOUR LOVE SHINE THROUGH
FOR ALL THE WORLD TO SEE

THERE'S NEVER BEEN A SISTER
THAT LOVES HER FAMILY SO
AND YOUR FAMILY LOVES YOU BACK
FOR EACH YEAR THAT YOU GROW

YOU HAVE TAKEN CARE OF OTHERS
ALL YOUR WHOLE LIFE THROUGH
IF YOU'RE NOT DOING NICE THINGS
YOU KNOW NOT WHAT TO DO

SO ON YOUR HAPPY BIRTHDAY
WE ALL WISH YOU A HAPPY DAY
GOD JOINS US IN SENDING LOVE
IN YOUR HEART TO FOREVER STAY

I NOTICED
by
Joseph Fram

I HAVE NOTICED LATELY
THAT THE OLDER THAT I GET
THINGS ARE HARDER TO REMEMBER
AND SO VERY EASY TO FORGET

I NOTICE THE STEPS GOT HIGHER
I REALLY DON'T KNOW WHEN
AND WHEN I TRY TO REMEMBER
THERE I GO AND FORGET AGAIN

I NOTICE WHEN I AM DOING THINGS
SOMETHING IS ALWAYS IN THE WAY
LIKE THE HOSE THAT JUST GOT TANGLED
ON THE CHAIR I MOVED THERE YESTERDAY

I NOTICE WHEN I AM WALKING
I TRIP ON THE SMALLEST THING
AND WHEN I WASH MY HANDS
I CANNOT REMOVE MY RING

YES I NOTICE ALL THE SMALL THINGS
FOR WHICH I'D NEVER PAID A WHIT
I HOPE IT'S JUST MY GROWING OLDER
AND NOT MY TURNING INTO A TWIT

OUR DREAMS

by
Joseph Fram

WHEN WE ARE YOUNG
OUR DREAMS ARE REAL
AND NONE CAN CHANGE
THE WAY WE FEEL

BUT AS WE GROW
THEY SOMETIMES FADE
WE CAN'T RECALL
THOSE DREAMS WE MADE

SOME PUT THEIR DREAMS
IN A PAGE THEY TURNED
IT CHANGED THEIR LIFE
FROM WHAT THEY LEARNED

STILL OTHERS KEEP
THEIR DREAMS INSIDE
WHERE THEY ARE LOST
AND HAVE SURELY DIED

ALAS, DREAM WE MUST
LEST WE LET THEM DIE
OR FOR THOSE WHO FOLLOW
WE HAVE LIVED A LIE

GOD'S CHOICE

by
Joseph Fram

GOD CHOOSES EACH ONE OF US
TO CARRY OUT HIS PLAN
CHANGING WHAT HE HAS IN MIND
IS NOT IN THE POWER OF A MAN

FOR SOME HE CHOOSES LEADERS
OTHERS TO FOLLOW AS THEY LEAD
EACH WITH COMFORT IN THEIR ROLE
THEY FILL EACH OTHERS' NEED

FOR SOME HE GIVES ALL RICHES
OTHERS TOIL THEIR WHOLE LIVES THROUGH
IF THEY WERE TO SWITCH THEIR ROLES
WOULD THEY THEN KNOW WHAT TO DO

OTHERS ARE PLACED HERE ON EARTH
WITH A MUCH DIFFERENT THOUGHT IN MIND
THEY DO NOT DO MOST WORLDLY THINGS
THEY ARE SENT TO BE GENTLE,
SWEET AND KIND

SO IT IS WITH DEAR ELIZABETH
WHO NEVER CLIMBED THE HIGHER HILL
SHE JUST BROUGHT JOY TO EVERYONE
SHE ONLY CARRIED OUT GOD'S WILL

THE OBVIOUS
by
Joseph Fram

WHEN WE OVERLOOK THE OBVIOUS
WE ARE SOMETIMES TOO INTENSE
WE FIX DON'T NEED FIXING THINGS
THAT REALLY DOESN'T MAKE MUCH SENSE

I RECALL AN ELECTRICAL PROBLEM
TO REPAIR WE DUG A DITCH
WHEN SUDDENLY THE LIGHTS WENT ON
SOMEONE THOUGHT TO THROW THE SWITCH

THEN THE TIME I SPENT HOURS
FILLING OUT SOME STORE REBATE
THEN I NOTICED AT THE BOTTOM
I SURPASSED THE EXPIRATION DATE

SOME ASSEMBLY MAY BE REQUIRED
QUICKLY BRINGS ME TO MY KNEES
I MUST OVERLOOK THE OBVIOUS
WHEN I WORK THEIR A'S AND B'S

AFTER YEARS OF MISPLACED EFFORT
I CAREFULLY READ EACH LITTLE THING
BUT I MUST OVERLOOK THE OBVIOUS
WITH EACH NEW FAILURE THAT THEY BRING

CHRISTMAS TREASURE
by
Joseph Fram

ONCE AGAIN IT'S CHRISTMAS
I SEE YOUR EYES ALL AGLOW
OUR HEARTS BOUND TOGETHER
FOR AS FAR AS WE GO

AT CHRISTMAS I MET YOU
WHEN I HAD NO TREE
GOD TOLD ME NO MATTER
AND SENT YOU TO ME

HE GAVE US BOTH A TREASURE
IN ALL THE LOVE THAT WE SHARE
AND ALL THE LITTLE THINGS WE DO
TO SHOW EACH OTHER THAT WE CARE

EACH DAY WE ARE TOGETHER
MY LOVE GROWS FOR YOU SOME MORE
AND YOU WILL KEEP GETTING
ALL THAT GOD KEEPS IN HIS STORE

SO TO YOU ALL MY LOVE
IS YOURS THIS CHRISTMAS DAY
ALONG WITH THE PROMISE
THAT IT WILL NEVER GO AWAY

A SCARE

by
Joseph Fram

OH, MY DEAR JESUS
I HAD SUCH A SCARE
WHEN MISFORTUNE BEFELL ME
I THOUGHT YOU WERE NOT THERE

MY MIND WAS KINDA HAZY
IT COULDN'T THINK SO CLEAR
I WAS NOT IN YOUR SHADOW
YOU WERE NOWHERE NEAR

ALL MY BURDENS YOU HAD CARRIED
AND STOOD CLOSE BY MY SIDE
WHEN I THOUGHT YOU HAD LEFT
I HAD FOUND NOWHERE TO HIDE

THEN I TOOK THAT MISFORTUNE
AS A MESSAGE YOU GAVE ME
THAT YOU LET ME KEEP ON LIVING
AND NOW CLEARLY I CAN SEE

SOMETIMES WHEN YOU SCARE US
IT IS THE TOUGHEST KIND OF LOVE
THAT WE MAY NOT BE LIVING
BY RULES SENT FROM UP ABOVE

BRAIN WASTER

by
Joseph Fram

DID YOU EVER BUY A PRODUCT
THAT DIDN'T WORK SO GOOD
YOU COULDN'T GET IT TO DO
WHAT THE SALESMAN SAID IT WOULD

WHEN YOU GOT IT HOME
NOT A THING YOU DID WAS RIGHT
AS YOU PREPARE TO RETURN IT
YOU EXPECT SOME KIND OF FIGHT

YOU TRY EACH WHICH WAY
TO MAKE THE DARN THING GO
YOU EVEN CALL THE FACTORY
ONLY TO HEAR AN "I DON'T KNOW"

YOU REHEARSE ALL THE REASONS
GET THEM ALL STRAIGHT IN YOUR MIND
ALL THE THINGS YOU WILL SAY
WHEN THAT TRICKY CLERK YOU FIND

THEN ALL YOUR EFFORT'S WASTED
YOU DON'T EVEN GET YOUR SAY
WHEN THE CLERK SMILES AND TAKES IT
WITH A HANDSHAKE AND AN "OK"

HOLD MY HAND
by
Joseph Fram

QUITE SOME TIME HAD PASSED
SINCE I PARTED FROM MY WIFE
I PREPARED TO STAY ALONE
SO THAT I COULD REPAIR MY LIFE

I HAD LOST MOST EVERYTHING
MY POSSESSIONS AND MY HEALTH
I COULD NOT IMAGINE ANYONE
WOULD WANT ME WITHOUT WEALTH

THEN ONE DAY I FOUND HER
SHE WAS SO KIND TO ME
SHE TOOK MY HAND AND SPOKE
OF HOW WONDERFUL LIFE COULD BE

I TOLD HER I AM NOT THE LOVER
THAT I USED TO BE
OF EVERYTHING WRONG
SHE SHOULD KNOW ABOUT ME

AFTER I HAD CONFESSED ALL
I TURNED TO WALK AWAY
"I NEED SOMEONE TO HOLD MY HAND"
I HEARD HER GENTLY SAY

MEXICAN BANK LINES

by
Joseph Fram

GET IN LINE WE WERE TOLD
THEY ONLY CASH CHECKS AT THE BANKS
THERE IS NOTHING ELSE YOU CAN DO
BUT WAIT HERE ALL DAY, THANKS

IT SEEMS SO STRANGE AND NEW TO ME
A LINE SO SLOW IT MAKES YOU AGE
SO MANY PEOPLE IN THE LINES
HOW DO THE CONTAIN THEIR RAGE

EACH CLERK IS HELPING SOMEONE
BUT THE BANK WILL CLOSE BY THREE
WELL, I ALREADY MISSED TWO MEALS
ONE MORE IS THE DEATH OF ME

ALL IN LINE SEEM SO CALM
SO WHY DO I COMPLAIN
I HAVE TWO MORE DAYS TO WASTE
BEFORE I MISS MY PLANE

BUT, GEE, I NEVER WOULD HAVE KNOWN
THE LIVES THESE PEOPLE LIVE
THEY SAY TIME IS ALL THEY HAVE
SO SOME OF MINE I NOW WILL GIVE

DOING NOTHING
by
Joseph Fram

I SPEND A LOT OF TIME THESE DAYS
DOING NOTHING SO IT SEEMS
BUT IT MAY CONTRIBUTE SOMETHING
TO MY LOST AND SHATTERED DREAMS

DOING NOTHING SEEMS THE ANSWER
WHEN I WAKE TO FACE THE DAY
AND IT ALSO SEEMS APPROPRIATE
WHEN TIMES I HAVE NAUGHT TO SAY

DOING NOTHING COMES IN HANDY
FOR A PROBLEM I CAN'T SOLVE
WHEN INSTEAD OF DOING NOTHING
ONLY PROBLEMS CAN EVOLVE

I THINK THAT DOING NOTHING
MANY TIMES AVOIDS A FIGHT
THAT WILL LEAVE FOREVER SCARS
NO MATTER WHO IS WRONG OR RIGHT

OH! I DO LIKE DOING NOTHING
IT STARTS AND ENDS WITH FUN
ONLY TROUBLE ABOUT DOING NOTHING
I NEVER KNOW WHEN I AM DONE

ONE MORE YEAR

by
Joseph Fram

WHAT A DIFFERENCE IN LIFE
JUST ONE YEAR CAN MAKE
IT CAN CHANGE OUR BODY AND MIND
BUT OUR LOVE IT CANNOT TAKE

HANDS THAT ONCE WERE STRONG
NOW GRASP FOR SOME AID
AGE REMINDS US THAT OUR BODY
HAS A PRICE THAT MUST BE PAID

BUT NO MATTER THE COST
WE HAVE OUR MEMORIES TO HOLD
AND THE PLEASURES THAT WE HAD
STAY YOUNG AND WILL NOT GROW OLD

GOD GAVE US SOME TIME
TO ENJOY THE TIME THAT WE HAD
WE NOW TREASURE EACH OTHER
THROUGH THE GOOD AND THE BAD

ENJOY EACH BIRTHDAY LITTLE DARLING
I AM WITH YOU TILL THE END
AS I TELL YOU SAME AS LAST YEAR
THAT MY LOVE WILL NEVER BEND

MOODS
by
Joseph Fram

SOMETIMES A WAVE OF SADNESS
TAKES HOLD OF THE SOUL IN ME
WHEN I LOOK IN THE MIRROR
I AM NOT THE MAN I USED TO BE

OTHER TIMES I TAKE A LOOK
AND THINGS ARE NOT SO BAD
I JUST WINK AND SMILE
FOR ALL THE THINGS I'VE HAD

IT IS HARD TO FIND A REASON
WHEN SOMETIMES I START TO CRY
THEN THE SAME THING MAKES ME LAUGH
I DON'T EVEN WONDER WHY

WHEN I AM IN ONE OF MY MOODS
I TRY TO ADJUST IT TO MY DAY
AND MAKE THE BEST OF GOOD OR BAD
I'VE FOUND IT THE MOST PRODUCTIVE WAY

I GUESS MOODS GO UP AND DOWN
THAT IS WHAT LIFE IS ALL ABOUT
WHEN I MEASURE GOOD AND BAD
THEY SEEM TO EVEN OUT

SHINE FROM WITHIN
by
Joseph Fram

WHEN JESUS PREACHED TO MANKIND
THEY LISTENED TO HIS EVERY WORD
BUT FROM WHAT THEY HAVE RECORDED
ONE WONDERS WHAT THEY HEARD

JESUS DID NOT ASK FOR TEMPLES
OR TO GATHER RICHES FOR HIS OWN
ANY GIFT THAT HE ACCEPTED
WAS CONSIDERED JUST A LOAN

JESUS' LESSON WAS OF LOVE
FOR ALL WOMEN AND EACH MAN
LOVE THAT IS FREELY GIVEN
WITHOUT A PRICE TAG OR A BAN

ALL THE TEACHINGS IN THE BIBLE
IN THE LORD'S PRAYER YOU CAN READ
IF YOU LIVE WHAT IT IS SAYING
THAT IS ALL THAT YOU WILL NEED

IN YOUR TIME OF WORSHIP
GRACE COMES FROM NOT ABOVE
IF YOU RELEASE THE SHINE WITHIN YOU
YOU WILL GLOW WITH JESUS' LOVE

WEEPING WILLOW
by
Joseph Fram

I WANDERED INTO WARSAW
NOT KNOWING WHAT I'D SEE
AND IN THE MIDST OF WARSAW
WAS THE WEEPING WILLOW TREE

EACH BRANCH CONTAINED A MEMORY
OF A SOUL LOST IN THAT LAND
WHERE MEN HAD KILLED EACH OTHER
AND LET THE WEEPING WILLOW STAND

WHERE THERE HAD BEEN SUCH HORROR
BECAUSE OTHERS LOOKED AWAY
WHILE NAZIS WALLED AROUND THE GHETTO
THE WORLD HAD NAUGHT TO SAY

SOME OF THEM FOUGHT BRAVELY
YET MANY HAD TO DIE
THE WEEPING WILLOWS MUST HAVE SENSED
IT WAS FOR HITLER'S FOOLISH LIE

THOUGH HISTORY IS OUR TEACHER
LESSONS LEARNED ARE FEW
WHEN I SAW THE WILLOWS WEEP
I ALSO STARTED WEEPING TOO

GOALIE GOB
by
Joseph Fram

GOALIE GOB TURNS SEVENTY-FIVE
I NEVER THOUGHT I'D SEE THE DAY
HE WAS HIT BY SO MANY PUCKS
HOW DIDN'T THEY BLOW HIM AWAY

AS I RECALL ONE FREEZING NIGHT
HE WAS KO'D -- IT IS NO JOKE
SCOTTY KNEW HOW TO BRING HIM BACK
WHEN HE ASKED "DO YOU WANT A SMOKE"

HIS LIFE IS CHARMED - HE AROSE
AND WOBBLED CAREFULLY OFF THE ICE
THEN HE REACHED FOR A CIGARETTE
AND SAID TO ME "NOW THIS IS NICE"

I DROVE HIM BACK TO HIS HOME
THROUGH SUCH FOG I COULD NOT SEE
I TOOK HIM TO HIS LOVELY WIFE
"WHAT HAPPENED NOW" SHE ASKED OF ME

IT'S JUST A STORY HE CAN TELL
AT A TIME WHEN HE GROWS OLD
I'M NOT SO SURE THIS IS THE TIME
HE GETS TO PICK WHEN IT BE TOLD

INSPIRATION

by
Joseph Fram

SOMETIMES SOMEONE WILL SAY THINGS
THAT JUST UPSETS ME SO
IT STIRS THOUGHTS IN MY MIND
YOU REALLY SHOULDN'T KNOW

THEN I STOP TO REFLECT A BIT
THAT IT COULD RUIN MY DAY
WHEN THEY HAVE LONG DEPARTED
I GUESS THEY HAD THEIR SAY

OH, I COULD THINK OF MANY THINGS
TO TELL THEM LATER ON
BUT WHY DO THESE THOUGHTS COME
AFTER THEY ARE LONG GONE

SO NOW I LEARNED A TRICK OR TWO
THAT MAKES MY DAY WORTHWHILE
INSTEAD OF GETTING ALL UPSET
WHAT THEY SAY JUST MAKES ME SMILE

THEY HAVE GIVEN ME AN INSPIRATION
TO WRITE A POEM OR TWO
ABOUT HOW FUNNY PEOPLE ARE
AND THE FUNNY THINGS THEY DO

POETS

by
Joseph Fram

ROMANCE IS A POET'S WORLD
THEY SEE WHAT OTHERS MISS
WHILE OTHERS MAY SEE CHAOS
THEY SEE PEACE AND BLISS

IN THEIR MINDS THEY CREATE A STORY
THAT OTHERS FAIL TO SEE
TRYING TO BRING PEACE AND CALM
AND LET THE MISERIES BE

THEY TAKE THE BEST IN EVERYTHING
A MEMORY SET IN STONE
FOR THE TIME WHEN LIFE IS UNFAIR
THEY WON'T BE ALL ALONE

OH, YES THEY SEE WHAT OTHERS DO
THEY COULD JOIN IN THEIR MISERY
BUT IF THEY DON'T PAINT THE ROSES
WHAT A SAD WORLD THIS WOULD BE

WHAT IS LIFE IF NOT A POEM
FOR EACH TO WRITE HIS OWN
WRITE THE PARTS THAT SUIT YOU
AND LEAVE THE REST ALONE

SOME BLAME IS MINE
by
Joseph Fram

NOW THAT I AM FAR AWAY
FROM INJUSTICES THAT WERE DONE
THERE ARE ONLY VAGUE MEMORIES
OF WHY THEY HAD BEGUN

I SEE THAT IN THE PROCESS
IT TAKES TWO TO MAKE A FIGHT
AND NEITHER ONE TO GIVE IN
SINCE BOTH THINK THEY ARE RIGHT

EVERY STORY HAS TWO SIDES
MOSTLY ONLY ONE IS HEARD
THE LOUDEST HAVE THEIR SAY
THE QUIET GET NO WORD

WHEN TWO LOVERS PART
THOUGH THAT LOVE HAS DIED
IT DOESN'T SEEM TO ME
IT'S BECAUSE THEY HADN'T TRIED

SO WHEN I STOP TO THINK
HOW I'VE GIVEN BLAME THAT'S THINE
THOUGH I CAN'T ASSESS THE PORTION
SOME OF THE BLAME IS MINE

MY AGING VALENTINE

by
Joseph Fram

TO MY AGING VALENTINE
THAT HAS BEEN MINE FOR VERY LONG
I HAVE LOVED YOU ALL THESE YEARS
THROUGH WHAT'S RIGHT AND WHAT IS WRONG

I CAN SEE SOME TATTERED EDGES
WHERE THE YEARS HAVE LEFT A TOLL
BUT I ALSO SEE THE MEMORIES
WHERE YOUR LOVE HAS PLAYED A ROLE

FOR WHEN YOU GET A VALENTINE
YOU LOVE IT FROM THE START
AND NO MATTER TATTERED EDGES
IT IS ALWAYS IN YOUR HEART

I CAN SEE THE FIRE TURNING EMBERS
AND SOME ASHES ALSO THERE
BUT I TREASURE ALL THE THINGS YOU ARE
AND OF THIS I HOPE YOU ARE AWARE

HAPPY VALENTINE'S DAY MY DARLING
TOGETHER A-TATTERING WE WILL GO
FOR ALL THE LOVE WE SHARE ETERNALLY
ONLY YOU AND I WILL EVER KNOW

CHORES

by
Joseph Fram

WE ALL HAVE OUR CHORES TO DO
SOMETIMES BIG AND SOMETIMES SMALL
SOMEHOW STUCK IN OUR MINDS
WE MUST COMPLETE THEM ALL

SOMETIMES THESE CHORES ARE NEEDED
SOME WERE ASSIGNED SO LONG AGO
BUT WE JUST CONTINUE DOING THEM
FOR REASONS WE STILL DO NOT KNOW

SOMETHING GIVEN BY OUR PARENTS
OR PERHAPS A TEACHER OR A NUN
SOME WE THINK WE HAVE TO DO
OTHERS WE DO JUST FOR THE FUN

AT SOME POINT WE STOP TO THINK
WHY ALL THESE CHORES FOR ALL THE YEARS
WE HEAR A VOICE FROM LONG DEPARTED
IF WE NEGLECT BRING CHILDHOOD FEARS

SO NOW I TAKE SOME TIME
TO EVALUATE EACH AND EVERY CHORE
AND BEFORE I DO EACH ONE
I ASK MYSELF WHAT I DO THIS FOR

THE DEED IS THE KEY
by
Joseph Fram

WHEN WE ARE HURT BY ONE THAT WE LOVE
OUR FIRST RESPONSE IS DISBELIEF
WE MAY CONDEMN THE PERSON FIRST
BUT THAT IS JUST FOR OUR RELIEF

WE KNOW THAT WE HAVE LOVED THEM
FROM THE TIME THAT WE FIRST MET
WE JUST DON'T UNDERSTAND THE ACT
AND HOW OUR LOVE THEY CAN FORGET

WE TRY TO GET INTO THEIR HEAD
AND PLACE OUR THOUGHTS IN THEIRS
BUT LATER ON WE REALIZE
THAT THOUGHTS DON'T COME IN PAIRS

BUT WE WANT TO KEEP THAT LOVE
WE KNOW THEY AREN'T ALL BAD
FOR IF IT WERE THE CASE
THIS LIFE WOULD BE SO SAD

SO TO KEEP A LOVE ALIVE
JUST CONDEMN THE DEED
HOPE THAT IT WILL NOT REPEAT
AND TO FORGIVENESS IT WILL LEAD

CHRISTMAS TOYS
by
Joseph Fram

I LOOKED AT ALL THE TOYS
I HAVE ACCUMULATED O'ER THE YEARS
THEY SHOULD BE BRINGING HAPPINESS
AND NOT SOME SENTIMENTAL TEARS

FOR EACH ONE THAT I HAVE
THERE IS A STORY TO BE TOLD
ABOUT ANOTHER TIME AND PLACE
YOU CAN'T RETURN WHEN YOU ARE OLD

THEY TALK OF THINGS I DID
WHEN I WAS IN MY PRIME
I'M LEFT WITH ONLY MEMORIES
FOR IT WAS ANOTHER TIME

BUT ALL IN ALL I'M SATISFIED
IT IS THE WAY I LIVE
THE ONLY THING THAT'S LEFT FOR ME
IS ALL THE LOVE THAT I CAN GIVE

CHRISTMAS HAS MORE MEANING NOW
THOSE TOYS ARE IN MY PAST
I PRAY THE LOVE THAT JESUS TAUGHT
THROUGH MY REMAINING YEARS WILL LAST

GOING ON NINETY

by
Joseph Fram

HELLO MY LITTLE CAROL
WHEN YOU WERE YOUNG, NINETY WAS OLD
YOU PROBABLY USED TO SCOFF WHEN
"YOU'LL GET THERE" YOU WERE TOLD

YOU'VE ALWAYS HAD AN EASY WAY
OF TURNING TROUBLES INTO SMILES
AND MAKING LIFE'S HIGHWAY
INTO FUN-FILLED MILES

YOU HAVE ALWAYS BEEN SO ACTIVE
YOU LEAVE YOUNGER ONES BEHIND
WHEN ONE ADVENTURE'S OVER
ANOTHER ONE YOU FIND

THERE ARE SO MANY THINGS YOU DO
TO HELP SENIORS AND THE YOUTH
THE KIDS IN MANY GRADE SCHOOLS
ATTEST TO THAT VERY TRUTH

NOW IT IS TIME TO SHARE YOUR DAY
AND SURROUND YOU WITH LOTS OF LOVE
I BET THAT GOD IS SMILING NOW
ON THE BIRTHDAY OF HIS TURTLE DOVE

WHEN A CUT LEAVES A SCAR
by
Joseph Fram

WHEN A CUT LEAVES A SCAR
LIKE A BADGE ON A FACE
IT IS ALWAYS REMEMBERED
APOLOGIES CANNOT IT ERASE

WHEN WORDS ARE SPOKEN
THAT CUT TO THE SOUL
THEY STAY THERE LIKE NAILS
YOU'RE NEVER AGAIN WHOLE

LIKE THE PEOPLE THAT TELL YOU
WHAT YOU ARE AND SHOULD BE
IT'S THE EVIL INSIDE THEM
IN YOU THAT THEY SEE

THEY KNOW ALL YOUR INTENTIONS
JUST WHAT YOU WILL DO
SO IN THEIR MIND'S EYE
YOU'RE ALL EVIL TOO

SO WHEN YOU LEAVE SCARS
THERE IS ONE THING TO KNOW
THE SCARS THAT YOU LEAVE
ALSO WITH YOU THEY WILL GO

PACKAGES

by
Joseph Fram

I ONCE HAD LITTLE PACKAGES
THAT CARRIED ALL MY PAIN
WHEN I FINALLY GOT THEM WRAPPED
I DID NOT WANT THEM OUT AGAIN

THOSE LITTLE PACKAGES THAT I HAD
WERE FROM ANOTHER TIME AND PLACE
WHEN I FINALLY LET THEM GO
I WAS FILLED WITH LOVE AND GRACE

ONE DAY YOU CAME UPON A PACKAGE
THAT HELD PIECES OF MY HEART
DO YOU REMEMBER LOOKING IN
AND ASKING ME "WHERE DO WE START?"

IT'S FUNNY HOW YOU TOOK THAT PACKAGE
WHERE ALL THE PARTS WERE STILL INSIDE
IT PLACED TOGETHER IN YOUR HANDS
WHERE YOU HAD HARDLY TRIED

WELL, NOW I HAVE MORE PACKAGES
BUT THEY ARE FILLED WITH JOY AND FUN
FOR WHEN YOU HELP ME TIE THE BOW
THERE IS LOVE IN EVERY ONE

IF I SHOULD DIE
by
Joseph Fram

IF I SHOULD DIE BEFORE I WAKE
I SOMETIMES THINK ABOUT
THAT IS WHY EACH NIGHT I HAVE
THREE PRECIOUS WORDS COME OUT

FOR MUCH IS SAID THROUGHOUT THE DAY
THAT REALLY DOESN'T MATTER MUCH
ABOUT THE SIMPLE THINGS WE DO
LIKE MUNDANE THINGS AND SUCH

ALL THIS WHILE WE SELDOM SPEAK
OF ALL THE LOVE WE SHARE
THOUGH EVEN IF IT IS NOT SPOKEN
WE KNOW THAT WE DO CARE

WHEN AT NIGHT BEFORE I SLEEP
I EXPECT TO SEE TOMORROW
AND FACE IT LIKE ANOTHER DAY
WITH ALL ITS JOY AND SORROW

BUT EACH NIGHT I ALSO THINK
I KNOW NOT WHAT GOD MAY DO
SO IF I DIE BEFORE I WAKE
MY LAST WORDS ARE "I LOVE YOU"

GOD'S ANGEL

by
Joseph Fram

GOD WAS SITTING AROUND ONE DAY
WITHOUT MUCH TO DO
TRYING TO CREATE AN ANGEL
BUT HE DIDN'T QUITE KNOW WHO

HE THOUGHT AND THOUGHT
OF ALL THE PEOPLE ON EARTH
AND HE PICKED OUT A BUNCH
BECAUSE HE VALUED THEIR WORTH

HE THOUGHT THEM TOO MANY
SO HE SAID "I'LL HAVE SOME FUN
OUT OF ALL OF THE ANGELS
I'LL PICK ONE SPECIAL ONE"

IT DIDN'T TAKE LONG
HE SAID "I KNOW WHO IT IS
MY ONE SPECIAL ANGEL
AND I WILL PICK MY 'LIZ'"

GOD'S ANGELS ALL ARE SPECIAL
I'M GLAD MY SISTER IS THE ONE
BUT I HAVE ANOTHER SISTER
SO I KNOW HE ISN'T DONE

WHAT USED TO BE
by
Joseph Fram

A CROWDED BEACH
THE BLUSH OF YOUTH
NOW DAWNS THE TIME
FOR INTERNAL TRUTH

FOR NOW I SEE
WHAT I USED TO BE
ALL THE THINGS THEY DO
WERE DONE BY ME

WOULD I EXCHANGE
MY LIFE NOW FOR THEN
PERHAPS, NOT LONG AGO
BUT NOW, NOT AGAIN

FOR BY MY SIDE
SITS MY LOVE ANEW
THAT WON'T COME AGAIN
100 LIFETIMES THROUGH

MY SEARCH IS O'ER
AFTER ALL THESE YEARS
I CAN FACE THE FUTURE
SHED OF ALL MY FEARS

I WONDER

by
Joseph Fram

SOMETIMES I SIT AND WONDER
WHEN THE FIRE WENT OUT OF ME
NOT ENJOYING THINGS I USED TO
OR THE BEAUTY IN THINGS I SEE

NOW DOING SOMETHING NEW
IS NOT WHAT I LOOK FORWARD TO
I WONDER WHY I JUST LIKE
ALL THE THINGS I USED TO DO

MAYBE IT'S IN THE TIME I LIVE
WHERE EVERYTHING YOU DO AND SAY
IS MEASURED BY A LAWYER'S TONGUE
WHO WILL TRY TO TAKE ALL AWAY

MAYBE BECAUSE I AM OLDER
THINGS DO NOT EXCITE ME SO
ALL THE DANGERS I ONCE LOVED
I FINALLY HAVE LET GO

I'M SURE THERE MUST BE SOMETHING
TO REKINDLE THE FIRE INSIDE ME
AND I GUESS I WILL KEEP ON SEARCHING
TILL I FIND WHATEVER THAT MIGHT BE

LITTLE GOLFER LADY
by
Joseph Fram

HERE'S TO LITTLE GOLFER LADY
CAROL HITS THEM DOWN THE MIDDLE
HOW SHE DOES IT EVERY TIME
TO ME REMAINS A RIDDLE

WHEN SHE HITS THAT NOODLE
AND IT DOESN'T TRAVEL LONG
SHE CALLS UPON DAYS GONE BY
BUT I LIKE TO HEAR THAT SONG

IT REALLY IS A PLEASURE
WHEN WITH HER I GET TO PLAY
FOR SHE IS GOING ON NINETY
WHERE I HOPE TO BE SOME DAY

SHE BOUGHT A DOZEN GOLF BALLS
I REALLY DON'T KNOW WHY
I DON'T RECALL HER LOSING ONE
SHE COULDN'T EVEN ON A TRY

SO ON HER NINETIETH BIRTHDAY
I'M GOING TO GIVE HER THREE
SHE WILL HAVE THE OTHER TWO
ON HER HUNDREDTH DON'T YOU SEE

OVER THE HILL
by
Joseph Fram

I SPENT MY LIFE A-WORKING
FOR THINGS I HAD TO BUY
LIKE FAMILY NEEDS AND EDUCATION
IT WAS AN UPHILL TRY

I HAD TO CLIMB THAT MOUNTAIN
FOR NEEDS THAT WOULD NOT STOP
AND THEN ENJOYED THE VIEW
WHEN I HAD REACHED THE TOP

WHEN YOUR JOURNEY LEADS UPHILL
YOU PUSH AND PULL TILL YOU ARE THERE
MOST GET TO THEIR DESTINATION
OTHERS MUST GO EVERYWHERE

WHEN WE HAVE REACHED OUR SUMMIT
IT'S OVER THE HILL WE GO
NOW WE DON'T HAVE TO PUSH AND PULL
AND WE CAN TAKE IT SLOW

REMEMBER WHEN YOU TAKE A TRIP
THE CLIMB IS THE HARDEST PART
AND COASTING ON THE OTHER SIDE
REWARDS YOU FOR YOUR START

FRAGILE PEOPLE
by
Joseph Fram

SOMETIMES WE HURT A FRAGILE PERSON
THAT WE HURT WON'T CROSS OUR MIND
WE NEVER STOP TO THINK
THAT WHAT WE SAY MAY BE UNKIND

OUR LIFE IS BUSY AND IMPORTANT
WE HAVE MANY THINGS TO DO
THE THINGS IN OUR LIFE ARE VITAL
IN THEIR LIFE VITAL IS VERY FEW

WE NEVER STOP TO THINK
FRAGILE ONES LISTEN TO EVERY WORD
THEY WILL REMEMBER YEARS FROM NOW
EVERYTHING THEY EVER HEARD

FRAGILE PEOPLE ARE ALWAYS SEEKING
WAYS TO GET THEM THROUGH THE DAY
WHEN WE SAY SOMETHING HURTFUL
IT IS THE FRAGILE THAT WILL PAY

WE GO ABOUT OUR BUSINESS
LIKE NOTHING'S HAPPENING THAT DAY
WE FORGET THAT FRAGILE PEOPLE
CLING TO EVERYTHING WE SAY

LIES

by
Joseph Fram

LIES ARE TOLD IN MANY WAYS
JUST TO GAIN SOME FAVOR
AND THE MORE ONE LIES EACH DAY
THE MORE HE HAS TO SAVOR

THERE ARE MANY KINDS OF LIES
AND DIFFERENT WAYS THEY ARE TOLD
SOME ARE SUBTLE AND YOU MISS THEM
OTHER ARE JUST DOWNRIGHT BOLD

SOME ARE TOLD WITH MANY WORDS
THEY SOUND LIKE THEY ARE TRUE
OTHERS BY WHAT IS NOT SAID
BUT WHAT THERE IS TO DO

SO WHEN YOU LIE THE FIRST TIME
YOUR SOUL IS BENT AND TORN
AND UPON YOUR SHIELD OF LIFE
FOREVER IT WILL BE WORN

SOMETIMES YOU THINK A LIE IS WARRANTED
TO SAVE ANOTHER FROM SOME SHAME
BUT I GUESS YOU SHOULD REMEMBER
IT IS A LIE JUST THE SAME

LOSING HOME
by
Joseph Fram

HOME TO ME HAS ALWAYS BEEN
A PLACE TO COME FOR PEACE AND QUIET
THE ONE PLACE YOU CALL YOUR OWN
WHERE NO OTHERS CAN DENY IT

THEN ONE DAY IT HAPPENS
YOUR WORLD IS TURNED UPSIDE DOWN
HAPPENSTANCE BEYOND YOUR CONTROL
BRINGS PEOPLE FROM ALL AROUND

ONE OF YOU NEEDS MORE HELP
THAN THE OTHER CAN PROVIDE
AND THE NEEDS GROW SO MUCH
EVENTUALLY YOU CAN'T HIDE

CARETAKERS COME TO THE AID
THEY DO WHAT THEY MUST DO
THEY HELP THE ONE THAT'S AILING
WITH NOT A THOUGHT FOR YOU

THAT IS WHEN YOU LOSE YOUR HOME
IT BECOMES A PLACE TO SLEEP
NOTHING IN IT IS A HOME
PEACE AT HOME WILL NEVER KEEP

WATCHING

by
Joseph Fram

WATCHING IS A HABIT
PRACTICED BY NEARLY EVERYONE
IT HAPPENS EVERYDAY
AND SOMEHOW IS NEVER DONE

WE WATCH THE MORNING SUN
AND THE SUNSET IN THE EVE
WE WATCH SOME AWFUL THINGS
LATER WE CANNOT BELIEVE

WE ALSO WATCH THE BEAUTY
OF A NEW LOVE WE UNFOLD
AND WE KEEP THE MEMORY
UNTIL WE ARE GRAY AND OLD

WE ALSO WATCH LOVED ONES DYING
WHILE PART OF US DIES TOO
WE'RE LEFT WITH ONLY MEMORIES
OF THE THINGS WE USED TO DO

THOUGH WE TREASURE MEMORIES
WHAT WE ARE IS NOT THE SAME
SO IF I CANNOT BE ALL TO YOU
I HOPE YOU HOLD ME NOT TO BLAME

WELL'S RUN DRY
by
Joseph Fram

I GOT TO THINKING
NO TOO LONG AGO
THAT I WASN'T THINKING
OR IT WAS MIGHTY SLOW

I GUESS I'VE BEEN THINKING
ABOUT THE SAME THOUGHT
THE SUBJECT'S EXHAUSTED
MORE THINKING BRINGS NAUGHT

I SHOULD CHANGE MY DIRECTION
THINK OF OTHER THINGS TOO
MAYBE EVEN EXPAND IT
WHY RESTRICT IT TO FEW

FOR THOUGHTS ARE LIKE WATER
YOU PUNCH A HOLE IN THE GROUND
YOU MUST KEEP ON LOOKING
TILL WATER YOU'VE FOUND

WHEN YOUR MIND'S EMPTY
NO NEED TO ASK WHY
YOU HAVE TO SEARCH ELSEWHERE
WHEN YOUR WELL HAS RUN DRY

QUITE A WHILE

by
Joseph Fram

IT TOOK ME QUITE A WHILE
TO SEE THE FACTS IN FRONT OF ME
THE PICTURES PAINTED IN MY MIND
WERE SORROW, GRIEF AND MISERY

I HAD LOST A LOVED ONE
I THOUGHT THE BLAME WAS MINE
I COULDN'T BRING MYSELF TO SEE
WHY I HURT AND SHE WAS FINE

I KEPT WRITING SCENES FOR HER
WHERE I WOULD BE THE HERO
SHE WAS GONE TO HER NEW WORLD
THOSE SCENES JUST NET ME ZERO

SHE WAS GONE I'D NOT LET GO
I HAD MY MIND CHAINED TO THE PAST
THEN FORGIVENESS BROKE THAT CHAIN
AND I WAS FREE AT LAST

YES, IT TOOK ME QUITE A WHILE
SOMETIMES GOD WORKS KINDA SLOW
HE DOESN'T HAVE TO HURRY NONE
TO WATCH HIS CHILDREN GROW

GOD CHOSE ME

by
Joseph Fram

GOD MADE ME THE WAY I AM
NO NEED TO CHANGE HIS CHOICE
NO MATTER HOW OTHERS TRY
I ONLY LISTEN TO HIS VOICE

I UNDERSTAND WHAT OTHERS SAY
I WATCH WHAT OTHERS DO
GOD COMES TO THEM IN DIFFERENT WAYS
I RESPECT THAT TOO

PERHAPS I MISSED A THING OR TWO
IN THE BIBLE THAT I READ
THE PART ABOUT LOVE FOR ALL
IS ALL ANYONE SHOULD NEED

WHY DOES IT TAKES SO MANY PAGES
TO SAY SUCH A SIMPLE THING
YOU DON'T HAVE TO BE AN OPERA STAR
IF ALL YOU WANT TO DO IS SING

MY SIMPLE PRAYER -- THY WILL BE DONE
THANK YOU FOR THE WAY I AM
I WILL NOT CHANGE WHAT YOU MADE OF ME
I SERVE EACH DAY THE BEST I CAN

CHOSEN MEMORIES
by
Joseph Fram

I TAKE ALL THOSE CHOSEN MEMORIES
AND SAVE THEM ONE BY ONE
I TAKE MY TIME IN DOING SO
UNTIL THE TIME THAT I AM DONE

EACH MEMORY THAT I TREASURE
TAKES ME TO ANOTHER TIME AND PLACE
SOMETIMES I DON'T REMEMBER DETAILS
BUT I CAN ALWAYS SEE A FACE

THE MEMORIES THAT I HARBOR
MAY NOT REFLECT AN ACCURATE ACT
LEAVING OUT THE BITTER PARTS
KEEPS PRECIOUS MEMORIES INTACT

NOT ALL MY MEMORIES ARE WANTED
SOME BRING BACK ACHES AND PAIN
THOSE ARE TEMPERED WITH FORGIVENESS
TO MAKE THEM CHOSEN ONCE AGAIN

I CANNOT CHANGE WHAT THINGS ARE DONE
OR AT THE TIME HOW IT PASSED
BUT I CAN FRAME MY MEMORIES NOW
TO MAKE EACH PRECIOUS MEMORY LAST

Have you read Volumes 1, 2 & 3
of Joseph's Journey?

- - - - - - - - - - - -

Coming Soon!

Joseph's Journey
Volume 5!

Take the next step
with Joseph in the journey of
a lifetime.

Books by Joseph Fram:

Joseph's Journey, Volume 1
Poetry of Hope, Help, Healing and Humor

Joseph's Journey, Volume 2
Psychological Concepts Expressed in Poetry

Joseph's Journey, Volume 3
A Look at the Flip Side of My Life

Joseph's Journey, Volume 4
A Look in My Rear View Mirror:
"Did I just Waste a Precious Life –
That Kept Mine from Being Used"

Copies of these books can be ordered by
sending your name and address with a
check or money order for $7.95 + $2.95
shipping & handling (total = $10.90 per
book) made payable to:

Everlasting Publishing
P.O. Box 965
Vancouver, WA 98666-0965

www.ingramcontent.com/pod-product-compliance
Lightning Source LLC
Chambersburg PA
CBHW071732020426
42331CB00008B/2000